STAYING SANE IN A CRAZY WORLD

CREATE YOUR PERSONAL STAYING SANE PLAN

JUDITH ASHLEY

Windtree Press

PRAISE FOR JUDITH ASHLEY

Judith Ashley's book has garnered praise from professional counselors, educators, and teachers, as well as from the general public.

"Judith Ashley has created a valuable tool for anyone wanting to take charge of their life. This short, but succinct little book, will help you design a plan for balance, positive thinking, action and personal responsibility."

Nancy D. Herrick, M. Ed, CTRTC,
Counselor Educator, Supervisor
US Representative, International Board of Directors, The William Glasser Institute
Co-author of *Take Charge of Your Life*, an International workshop

"This is a short book but packed with good information about focusing on what you can and can't control. It provides a way for you to develop your own plan to keep you going every day. The author asks good questions to consider and leads you through the process of looking at the world in a different perspective and by the end you can feel that you are not lost in a world out of control."
—Maggie McVay Lynch, Ed.D.

really like a fun, but informative book. " — **Christine Woinich, Kobo Books Reviewer**

"This book was birthed out of the author dealing with her staying sane when her world was chaotic and crazy. The purpose of the book was give information that anyone has capacity to stay sane if they have a plan. Judith lays out in great detail the components required in developing one's personal plan. Judith is saying, look people, I had a time when my world was rocked and turned upside down. Based on my training and working in social services, in addition to my years of being a facuity member of the William Glasser Institute, I developed a plan that brought sanity to my crazy world. Here it is, use it to bring sanity to your crazy world."
— **Richard Sharp, CTRCT**

"This is a very easy to read how to book. I love that the author keeps it simple and uses or offers some realistic measures to make it happen. Great tools for success. Author also doesn't pretend to have all of the answers but merely offers some assistance to real life occurrences.
My first read of this type from this author and finding it useful is a plus." —**Teri, Goodreads Reviewer**

"In this short but powerful book, Judith Ashley provides practical foundational techniques for determining what's important to you and guidance on setting up a plan to create balance and joy in your own life regardless of what's happening around you. A great reminder that we have the ability to make conscious choices to create the life we want to live." — **Connie Cole, Amazon Reviewer**

"It is rare for me to read non-fiction. When I was offered to read this book I didn't know what to expect. It did sound interesting. I know how crazy the world can be and sometimes saying sane is really difficult. So, I wanted to know what is author's take on the issue. It did not disappoint me. Everything is logical and it does work. Unconsciously that's exactly what I've been doing, I just didn't know there was a method to it all. Yes, I can personally attest that this approach works. It's all here you just need to follow the plan and maybe then you will find a little balance in life. Best thing is that it's for everyone. It doesn't matter what yo believes are you can make it your own. Do it your way becau there are no absolute rights or wrongs here just our own per tion of the world we live in." — **Fizza Younis, Amazon Reviewer**

"This is one great book. Those days when your min and you are going in circles this is a book that hel finding what you need to learn to get a handle understand and follow. I enjoyed it and will

CONTENTS

1.	Why This Book?	1
2.	Your Core Values are Key	5
3.	What is a Crazy World?	11
4.	Control or No Control	17
5.	Where Do You Find the Courage of Acceptance?	21
6.	Decide What You Can Control/Change	25
7.	What You Can Do With A Little Control	35
8.	Finding Balance in A Crazy World	39
9.	Staying Sane Spiritual Practices	45
10.	Modifying Your Plan	49
11.	Wisdom To Choose Your Path	53
12.	Change and The Grieving Process	55
13.	Revisit Your Core Values	67
14.	My Personal Staying Sane Plan	71
15.	Staying Sane - update	75
16.	Example: Judith's Staying Sane Plan - 02/2018	81
17.	Another Format Option for My Staying Sane Plan	85
18.	Example: My Revised Plan:	87
19.	Criteria for a Good Plan	89
20.	YOUR Personal Staying Sane Plan	93
21.	Alternative Format for YOUR Personal Staying Sane Plan	95

Bonus Material	99
New Non-Fiction By Judith Ashley	107
Fiction by Judith Ashley	109
Connect with Judith	111
Acknowledgments	113
About Judith	115
Windtree Press	117

Copyright © 2018 by Judith Ashley.

All rights reserved. No part of this publication may be reproduced, distributed or transmitted in any form or by any means, including photocopying, recording, or other electronic or mechanical methods, without the prior written permission of the publisher, except in the case of brief quotations embodied in critical reviews and certain other noncommercial uses permitted by copyright law. For permission requests, write to the publisher, addressed "Attention: Permissions Coordinator," at the address below.

Windtree Press

www.windtreepress.com

Cover Design: Christy Keerins

http://Coversbyclkeerins.com

Staying Sane/Judith Ashley -- 1st ed.

EBOOK ISBN 978-1-947983-35-9

PRINT BOOK ISBN 978-1-947983-36-6

 Created with Vellum

Thank you to the women who share the Dark of the Moon with me each month. It is because of your willingness to share your journey with me that this book has come into being.

1
WHY THIS BOOK?

I was driving on the freeway to an appointment when a picture popped into my mind – a vivid picture of a golden haired woman, her arms raised in prayer, the sun shining down on her creating a halo effect. In that same moment the title to this book also popped into my head. Energy poured through me as images and ideas solidified into *Staying Sane in a Crazy World*.

I can do this! This is my book to write!

In those moments of discovery I levitated – well, not really because my seat belt held firm – but energetically I was flying high!

That was in September. I was working on the ending of *Visions of Happiness*—a spin-off from *Lily*, the first book in The Sacred Women's Circle series.

The landscape blurred as I sped down the freeway and I made a commitment to myself to start *Staying Sane* as soon as I finished *Visions*.

Then, as can happen to all of us, life interrupted.

I was still excited about writing this book but Life interceded during October. That month I did start it, writing almost one thousand words in the dark of the night when I couldn't sleep.

LIFE hit hard in November. One night in the wee small hours, when sleep eluded me, I opened the manuscript, read it through, and tweaked a few places before heading back to bed. All in all I didn't make much progress.

December arrived and I realized my goal of having this book written and published by the end of November obviously had not happened. Would it even be done by the end of December?

I didn't know the answer to that question but I did know:

- I still felt passion when I thought about writing this book.
- The first step to writing a book is just that – put words on the page and write the book!
- I had stayed sane during a couple of very crazy months in what to me was a crazy world.

It's a new year and here I am, again at the computer putting new words on the page.

My goal is to give you information you can use to create your own *Staying Sane in a Crazy World* plan.

The key to this working is *You*. You are the one to customize a plan that fits *You*. Your lifestyle, your interests, your beliefs, your spirituality, your core values is what makes your Staying Sane Plan work for you.

2

YOUR CORE VALUES ARE KEY

Before you start creating your *My Personal Staying Sane Plan*, it's important to understand Core Values. Core Values are those beliefs that are so integrated into us, they color our view of ourselves and the world around us. At the end of this book, I've included a chapter on where our core values originate. Knowing that is a bonus but not critical to you formulating your *My Personal Staying Sane Plan*.

Core Values are often seen by us as "The Truth" and because they are "The Truth," it isn't unusual to for people to assume everyone else shares their Core Values or should because, after all, they are "The Truth."

That perspective is at the center of many, if not most, of the difficulties we have with ourselves and other people.

When applied to ourselves, the phrase I use is *being out of integrity*. Whether the problem is within ourselves or with others, there is a disconnect between what is happening and one or more of our Core Values. And the other people part of the equation? "They" make decisions that are not in line with "our" Core Values which are, if you will recall in the previous paragraph, "The Truth." Therefore "they" are wrong.

Core Values are our moral compass and point us in what, for us, is the right direction. It's very difficult to accept when we are right that there can be another point of view that is also right.

However, if one of our Core Values is that everyone has their own Core Values and they are most likely a little or a lot different from our own—and that's okay, we eliminate a large obstacle from our own sanity.

In addition to understanding our Core Values, it's imperative we accept personal responsibility for our choices if we truly want to stay sane. It is only through the power of personal choice that we have the power to choose sanity.

Personal choice means we accept that we are responsible for our lives, including the positive and less positive aspects that are woven into the fabric of our day-to-day world.

It is this acceptance or even embracing of our personal responsibility that gives us the power to make different choices and thus change the direction of our lives.

Some of these concepts may sound familiar, especially if you are acquainted with the work of world renowned psychiatrist, Doctor William Glasser. I've been involved with The William Glasser Institute since 1978 and I'm on the teaching faculty for the organization. My signature line on emails within the organization includes "Your Choices Today Create Your Tomorrow."

Because this is one of my Core Values it means it is true for me. It also fits well with the concepts put forth in *The Law of Attraction* and *The Secret* and numerous books, CD's, movies, videos and workshops that have as a Core Value the concept we are in control of our lives, and we have to make new choices if we want our lives to be different.

Another aspect of the main message is that to have what we want in our lives, our focus needs to be on the positive of what we want. Our language, the words we use to describe what we want, is critically important.

Listen to yourself when you talk. Do you use negative words? Does it sound like you are complaining?

I don't want to be in debt or I wish I had more money is not the same as *I have financial security*. Or,

Each month I easily pay my financial commitments and put at least $100.00 into savings.

I want to feel better or to have better health is not the same as *I am fit and flexible and at my perfect weight*. Or,

I can walk a mile in ten minutes, touch my toes and weigh (put in your perfect weight).

∽

When I was in my thirties, I attended a workshop that challenged my view of the world. I was asked "How did I know something was true?"

An example: How did I know I couldn't afford to buy a house? *What is interesting to me, is that shortly after that workshop I decided to check out whether I could afford to buy a house. I've just passed my forty-second year in the house that, when I took that workshop, I believed I couldn't afford.*

Initially in my work as a child protective service worker, I believed anyone who mistreated a child was a bad person. That actually was counter to my Core Value that people are intrinsically good. I was experiencing two sides of the same coin.

When I stopped and looked at the situations I investigated I could see that the person who was abusive was doing their best. Their best didn't ensure their child's safety but they did not get up in the morning thinking about what they could do to harm their child.

In truth, they did not have the resources or parenting skills to be a better parent. Because of that realization I never challenged a parent on whether they loved their child.

You might ask how anyone could abuse a child or anyone they profess to love?

Here is my answer.

Love can be described as an emotion, a feeling.

Love can also be described by our actions. It is totally possible to "feel" love and yet not "act" in a loving way.

And when we are acting in an unloving way, one of our Core Values is involved.

Examples:

We have a Core Value of ourselves as good parents but then our child has a temper tantrum at the grocery store. The reality of how our child is behaving is not congruent with our perception of our self as a good parent—if we use our child's actions as our measurement.

We have a Core Value that if someone loves us they would always respect us. Within our concept of respecting us, that means they would always let us know if there is a change in plans such as a meeting going long, being late for a date, dinner, etc.

You and your partner could both have a Core Value of showing each other respect. You could have discussed this topic committing to being respectful of each other.

Now you've waited at the restaurant for an hour, you expect your partner any moment. When the other person shows up, you may not greet her or him in the most loving and kind way.

That depends on two things: did you both define what "respect" meant, describe situations like a meeting running late, caught in traffic and what you would each do to show respect to the other person?

Or do you have a Core Value that everyone is doing their best or at least trying to do their best at all times?

Depending on how specific you both were in your

communication about respect and your Core Value about people doing their best, you will greet your partner differently than if you take it as a personal affront, a sign of disrespect that you were left waiting.

It is all about you and how you see the world that determines what you will do in these circumstances.

In the next chapter, I list some of my Core Values as well as some of the sanity challenging situations I encounter in my life.

It's also time for you to begin creating your own *Personal Staying Sane Plan*. If you haven't already, get paper, pen (different colored inks or highlighters) OR if you are paperless, an electronic device where you can enter data.

Ready? Let's get started.

3
WHAT IS A CRAZY WORLD?

Where shall we start?

Our foundation is "The Serenity Prayer" by Reinhold Neibuhr (1892 – 1971). Go ahead and Google "Serenity Prayer" if you haven't read it recently or haven't even heard about it. When you do, you may learn "The Serenity Prayer" is a foundational element of Twelve Step Programs.

Now you may wonder or even question why start with "The Serenity Prayer" especially if you don't have addiction issues?

The answer is simple. The truth of "The Serenity Prayer" is perfect for your *My Personal Staying Sane Plan.*

We are blending "The Serenity Prayer" with world-renowned psychiatrist Dr. William Glasser's "Procedures That Lead To Change."

First up is "The Serenity Prayer." Here we are asked to do our own self-reflection and make choices based on what we find, what we see (what our Core Values are). The final line in the prayer is about having the wisdom to know the difference between what we can change and what we cannot change. For the purpose of this book, I'm adding the word *control* – what we can and cannot control.

On these pages, we'll talk about specific things we can do to reclaim our sanity, find a purpose that brings us joy and thus create our individual plan to stay sane even when or in spite of the world around us going crazy.

But first we have to **identify what in our world or in our life is Crazy?**

There is more than one way to do this. What works best for me is to take a look at my Core Values. Everything that appears crazy to me is something that bumps up against one or more of my Core Values.

Core Values are things like respect, honesty, dignity, equality, etc. Think Boy Scout motto for more.

However, Core Values are more than a word or short phrase. Each of us have our own picture or scenario of what that Core Value looks like when manifested.

In an earlier example I used "Respect." How do you know when someone respects you? What do you do to show someone you respect them? When is it okay to not show someone respect? If we were in a group and compared notes there would be some words, phrases, scenarios that would be similar or even the same. However, we each would have at least one thing we would do differently than others in our group.

Here are some of my Core Values:

Spiritual: Earth, The Universe is sacred. Everything including us is part of The Divine.

Friendship: I have very clear ideas on what friendship entails, what my contribution is and what I expect from others who are friends. I have a hierarchy that goes from acquaintances where I have very few expectations to Very Best Friend where my expectations are more. I will admit that over the years, I have modified even my expectations for VBFs because my Core Value that everyone is doing his or her best given what's going on in their lives has taken precedence. In other words, it isn't all about me.

Freedom: Each one of us on this planet is entitled to freedom of spiritual practice, freedom from fear, freedom to express themselves as long as that expression does no harm to others.

Respect/Dignity: Every person deserves to be treated with dignity and respect regardless. I know I'm being treated with respect when I'm being listened to, treated in a kind way, etc. *I could go into more detail because the words "listen" and "kind" also have their own scenarios.*

There is enough. This has been slightly altered to now

say, if we are mindful of the environment, there is and always will be enough

Peace: Treating others with kindness, a smile, a wish for all in their world to go right is my way of supporting peace on earth.

Your list of Core Values can be as general or as specific as you want to make it. What's important is that you recognize, if you use a word or phrase, that it has a special meaning for you that might not be the same for someone else who uses the same word or phrase.

Once you have made your list of Core Values, on a separate sheet of paper, write down what you see in the world around you that is "crazy".

Be thorough.

My list includes:

---**Negative, narrow-minded people**

---**News broadcasts**

---**Politics**

+ **Publishing**

+ **Sexual "Misconduct"**

+ **Social media**

And yes, I did reorder them so they'd be in alphabetical order – not that I'd be crazy if they weren't but I like it better this way.

I listed broad categories but the truth is there are any number of individual examples under each. Include as much detail as you want.

Once your list is as complete as you can make it for now review the list. *Things will come up and as this is a living breathing list, changes will occur. Cross off or add items as it benefits you.*

An example from my own life. I have two long- time friends who now have dementia. While they still know me, neither is able to have the in-depth or philosophical discussions we used to have. And for various reasons, we no longer go out for a meal or social event.

My Core Value about myself as a friend includes my staying in the friendship as best I can. That will still be true for me, even when they no longer recognize me.

They have changed and will continue to change in their cognitive functioning which is why my expectations of them has changed. However, my Core Value, how I see myself as a Best Friend has not.

As you review your list, create a system that works for you so you can identify the following:

Where you have no control.

Where you do have control.

Ideas include: highlighting with different colored markers; using a distinctive mark such as an *** by them or, if typing, you can change the font.

What's important is that you can easily see the difference between the two categories.

4

CONTROL OR NO CONTROL

CONTROL OR NO CONTROL THAT IS THE QUESTION

"The Serenity Prayer" asks us to Accept the Things I Cannot Change. But first, let's step back and double-check our list.

My list includes:

---**Environmental challenges like fires, earthquakes and hurricanes**

---**Negative, narrow-minded people**

---**News broadcasts**

---**Politics**

+++**Publishing**

+++**Sexual "Misconduct"**

+++**Social media**

I've used --- to show what I have no control over and thus cannot change and +++ to show what I do have control over.

I'm also going to add **housework** to my +++ list because, as you will soon see, just because we have control doesn't mean we do it. And in truth, if we don't do it, our life can become chaotic if not actually crazy.

Now that you've clearly listed what you can and cannot change, review each item and ask yourself "Is that true? Am I sure there is nothing I can do?"

In 2017 the Northwest of the United States had one of the worst forest fire seasons ever. While I cannot change that, there are some things I can do that might mitigate the issue of unseasonably high temperatures and tinder dry vegetation.

Here are the first three ideas that came to mind:

1. *I can pay attention to my own actions when out in nature.*
2. *I can pay attention to the actions of others and speak out if I see someone engaging in or doing anything that might endanger the forest.*
3. *I can write and/or call my congressional representatives and encourage them to support funding for appropriate forest management.*

I invite you to go through your list of **Things I Cannot Change and Over Which I Have No Control.** Look at this list with a creative and open mind while asking the question: *What might I be able to do?*

Politics is a Big Category for me. At first glance, other

than voting, what do I have control of? More than I'd originally thought. When I asked myself *What Can I Do?* I knew I could become more active locally.

A memory of speaking out at a town hall type meeting in the 70's came to mind. The state legislator who was answering questions came up to me afterward and encouraged me to run for my state legislature. I chose not to for a wide variety of reasons.

But it is now 2017 and I'm not working an 8 – 5 job and raising children. So what can I do now?

~~~ Attend my Neighborhood Association meetings. Because I have been a faithful attendee, I was asked to serve as a Board Member-At-Large. I feel better because I am doing something instead of complaining or bemoaning or criticizing.

~~~ Another place I'm active on the local level is a neighborhood meeting focused on public safety.

~~~A third place? I volunteered to re-energize my block's Neighborhood Watch.

~~~And last but not least I read my neighborhood newspaper *The Star* in order to be more informed about what is going on in my piece of the world.

In these small ways I'm engaging with the powers-that-be, speaking up and voicing my opinions and encouraging others to become part of the solution(s).

Take the time to go through your list and mark those issues where you can see a way to participate.

+ On the national scene you may decide to write, email, phone, text your congressional representatives and the White House with your opinions about legislation, policy, etc.

+ You may see that joining an organization that supports your point of view and adding your membership dues, donations and voice is a better fit for you.

What's important is for you to choose which action step will work best in your plan.

And if you find you do not want to do anything, that's okay. Just make note of it and acknowledge to yourself, if not others, why that is.

5
WHERE DO YOU FIND THE COURAGE OF ACCEPTANCE?

"The Serenity Prayer" encourages us to Accept The Things I Cannot Change and asks for the Courage to Change The Things I Can.

The reality is there are things we cannot change.

---Environmental challenges like fires, earthquakes and hurricanes

---Negative, narrow-minded people

---News broadcasts

---Politics

+++ Publishing

+++ Sexual "Misconduct"

+++ Social media

I've already talked about the first item on my list and

while I have no direct control, I listed a few things I can do to prevent or help in the aftermath.

Let's look at my second --- item. **Negative, narrow-minded people.** Since I come from the point of view that I cannot control anyone except myself, this stays in the red column. Accepting that there will always be negative people who are dissatisfied with their lives, relationships and the world around them takes some effort on my part because I know that doesn't have to be true. What is also true is that we do not change unless we want to.

This is my plan:

First I do engage to see if the person is open to seeing the situation from a different perspective. Right now, where I live, homelessness is a big issue.

Some vocal people see every homeless person as mentally ill, addicted and criminal. To be fair, maybe they don't see every homeless person with all three but they do see them with at least two of the three labels.

Having worked with people who are homeless that is not my perspective. I'll point out a couple of facts but that is all. If the other person is committed to their point of view, I step away.

What I do next comes from my own spiritual practice. I close my eyes, take a deep breath, exhale slowly and envision the person surrounded in white light and I send them peace and love in the form of prayer or energy.

Another way I deal with my perspective of **negative**

narrow-minded people is through wise compassion. Truly, I actually can't imagine what it would be like to live moment-by-moment with all that fear and hate. So I do feel compassion for that person.

However, wise compassion is different from what we usually mean when we use the word "compassion." Wise compassion seeks to understand the other person and understand the pain they are experiencing but we do that without joining in.

What's important is that you find a way to accept and be at peace with those things over which you have no control and thus cannot change.

You may find a Core Value that is useful to you at this point. Here are some sayings that reflect Core Values.

"Let go and Let God."

"We are never given more than we can handle."

"Trust that all is unfolding as it is meant to."

"This too shall pass."

"Time heals all wounds (physical, mental and emotional)."

What would you add to this list?

6

DECIDE WHAT YOU CAN CONTROL/CHANGE

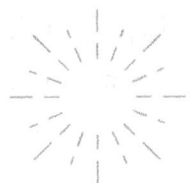

Let's move on to the next step which is identifying what we can change. Those items have +++ to identify them.

---Environmental challenges like fires, earthquakes and hurricanes

---Negative, narrow-minded people

---News broadcasts

---Politics

+++ Publishing

+++ Sexual "Misconduct"

+++ Social media

+++ Housework

Because we do have control over something and therefore can change it doesn't mean that we do. Blocks to our taking action vary but I've found that the basic ones include: the task isn't fun, it's hard; and, built into that perception is the fear of failure.

When there is something that is fun and easy competing for our attention, unless we have our plan in place, we usually don't move forward. Some of us call this procrastination.

Take the time to go through your list of "Over Which I Have No Control." Think creatively about what you can and cannot do. Know that there are some things we tell ourselves we can't do that we actually can do if we put the time, effort and energy into it. When you come to those items, you may want to mark them in a different way by saying to yourself, "this isn't important enough to me to put the time, effort and energy into it" and then set it aside.

Understand that the feelings of helplessness and hopelessness are fertile ground for slipping into the dark despair of craziness that can be a piece of living in a crazy world.

As you separate out your list, you'll see there is a difference between those items and the ones where you really have no control or power to change.

Once you've done that, it is time to put the list "Over Which I Have No Control/Cannot Change" to one side.

Why? Because your **My Personal Staying Sane Plan** is focused on your "What I Can Control/What I Can Change list."

Don't be surprised if, at this point, you already find yourself feeling better. The world may still be crazy but you now see a spot of light, of sanity within it.

By keeping our attention on Staying Sane even when the world around us is crazy we focus on those things we can change and over which we do have control. I guarantee you will feel better once you are making progress on this list even though the world around you may still be crazy.

So here's my curated list:

+++ **Publishing**

+++ **Sexual "Misconduct"**

+++ **Social media**

+++ **Housework**

What works best for me is to use a continuum with tasks that take little time and little effort on one end and the more overwhelming tasks that will take time, effort, energy on the other.

If that works for you, great!

If it doesn't, then organize the tasks in a way that works for you.

I'm starting with an easy to do task over which I have complete control that creates chaos and thus craziness in my personal world.

Housework. Notice I use the term 'housework' not 'housekeeping.'

Since I dislike housework, I'd have things like dusting, mopping floors on one end. I can do these things. I have control over doing them. I just don't like doing them so I procrastinate and then these simple tasks become more onerous because they will take up much more time, effort, energy to complete due to my neglect when days, weeks, months have passed.

Time for a confession: While I do not like housework, I do know people who gain a great deal of satisfaction from cleaning. I get a great deal of satisfaction from *seeing* things clean but that isn't the same thing.

At one point I made a plan to clean one refrigerator shelf each week. I envisioned the sparkling clean refrigerator, dutifully cleaned one shelf and then—nothing. The next week nothing got cleaned. I told myself, one shelf had taken hardly any time. Next week I'll do two shelves.

You may already know that the next week came and lo and behold, no refrigerator shelves were cleaned.

As I write this, my refrigerator is sparkling clean because my daughter-in-law and her sister spent about an hour and got it done. I was there at the time checking the contents as they were pulled out. Lemon curd with an expiration date of 2014! was only one item that ended up being tossed.

What I've accepted is that I will never love much less like housework. With that realization, I have some options:

~Live in a filthy house.

~Ask family to help or to just do the cleaning for me.

~Hire someone to do the cleaning on a regular basis.

I'm not willing to accept the first option. When I started writing this book I was doing more of the second one. As I'm finishing it, I've moved to the last. I've hired someone to clean my house!

I already do that with my yard and it is well worth the price to have the weeds pulled, the drip system turned on in the spring and off in the fall by someone who is confident in the process. Since I love geraniums and fuchsias there is always something I can do if I must get out and "play" with the plants.

In my own defense, I do take care of several indoor plants. I see that they are watered, dead leaves and blooms removed, turned to evenly get the sun and other tasks that keep them happy and healthy.

Take some time—you may need a day or two to cull through your list and see what creative solutions you can come up with. Here are a few housework suggestions:

Clean a room a week. Similar to my clean a refrigerator shelf a week, one room may not seem as daunting.

Turn on your favorite music and dance your way through the tasks.

Job share: invite a friend to help you with the task you like least (mine would be dusting) in return you will help her/him with a similar task.

Treat yourself to something special for finishing the task.

Tell more than one person, perhaps even announce it on Facebook or Twitter or Instagram that you are going to complete the task. Ask for ideas, suggestions to make it more palatable, easier or fun.

Now that we've explored my housework issues, let's look at +++ Publishing which is first on my "Can Change/Can Control" list.

With Indie Publishing being a viable option, I do have control of seeing my books published. If you check out my website http://judithashleyromance.com you'll see that I'm multi-published in romantic women's fiction.

However, any author will tell you there is more to publishing than writing your book whether you are indie or traditionally published.

To be multi-published I've had to learn software programs, create accounts with e-book distributors. I've also learned about author pages, meta-data, SEO.

I've searched photo data bases for cover art, learned the basics of creating a book cover, planned weekly and monthly and guest blog posts, and learned how to do all of the related essential tasks: copy/paste, upload/schedule, insert/embed well you get the picture.

Writing the books has been easy in comparison to what I need to learn and do in the ever growing, changing area of promotion and marketing.

This is where the rubber of the "yes, I have control and can change things" meets the road.

There are people who are more technologically wired than I am. My two and a half year old great-granddaughter can use a smart phone better than I can but that does not mean I can't.

It just means it takes a bit more effort for me. In addition it is critically important for me to not criticize myself or do those mental eye-rolls as I embark on a new techie learning curve.

After all, I am intelligent. I've proven I can conquer techie things (I've co-founded Romancing The Genres International Group Blog with Sarah Raplee, I've indie published seven full-length novels, I contributed to three and assisted in the publishing of two anthologies, etc.).

In other words I'm not the new kid on the block – however, even with all that I've done to date, technology does not come easy for me.

My Staying Sane Publishing Plan includes the following steps:

1. Stay calm – when feeling stressed, save what I'm working on and walk away.
2. Small steps – break the major task down into pieces so small they appear easier.
3. Face the fear – the computer most likely will not explode when you click on something to download a program or plug in your webcam. In my case I worried to the point of fearing I'd damage my computer if I plugged in my new webcam the wrong way. It took me six months after I purchased it before I took the plunge. And yes, now I can almost smile about it – at the

time it was not funny which is why it's important to:

4. Keep a sense of humor.
5. Be kind, gentle and respectful with myself both in thought, word and deed. And this one ties back into #1.

When I feel stressed and frustrated, I save my work, get up and leave the computer entirely. I may come back to the computer later to work on another project (like writing or checking emails, etc.) but until I'm back in the calm place, I do not go back to the technical project.

And sometimes, I need to re-evaluate my process. It's entirely possible that what looked like a small step is actually much larger as I work on it than I thought it would be as I made my list.

Another tactic is to intersperse publishing tasks I love (like writing) with those tasks that do not appeal to me. As I move onto a more focused path of marketing and promotion, I know it is important to keep writing new words on new stories. It's also important to stay connected to my writing buddies, those other authors who understand the challenges of being an indie author.

The option I keep open is to hire someone to do the work.

I've checked out hiring a Virtual Assistant – but I still

have to write the blog post, article, etc. So I keep doing the writing and scheduling.

A few years ago, I took a cover design class and a year ago I learned Canva (software to make covers and other graphic products) through an on-line class. However, since I almost get hives thinking of searching for pictures, colors, etc. I'd much rather hire that out and save my time, effort and energy for a task that may be onerous but doesn't have hive-producing possibilities.

7

WHAT YOU CAN DO WITH A LITTLE CONTROL

The second item on my "Control Over" list is +++ Sexual Misconduct. Over my fifty years working in social services, I have worked in the child welfare system, the women's section of a county jail, in domestic and international adoption as well as in an After Hour's emergency response program for vulnerable adults. I am a member of the #MeToo movement. Why is this important? Because I've seen the effects of sexual abuse whether of children or adults.

What is important to me with +++ Sexual Misconduct is to remind myself of what I professionally know. And that is I've never talked to a boy, girl, man or woman who shared a story of sexual abuse that was a lie.

What I also know is that some tell an abbreviated version

of what happened to see what the response of others will be. They've learned, usually from experience, that it isn't safe to talk about what happened to them.

What I know is true is that at some point in their lives they were assaulted. Perhaps they told someone and weren't believed, or told someone and were blamed for the assault, or told someone and were punished as if it was their fault.

The teenage girl might not have been assaulted by the foster father, but she was assaulted by someone.

In my child welfare work, I also never met a mother of a sexually abused child who had not also been abused as a child herself. I am certainly not saying that every mother of a sexually abused child is also a survivor of child sexual abuse, only that everyone in my caseloads over the years were.

So my first step is to recognize that what is being reported happened as it is being reported or something similar happened.

What is a challenge in this area is when someone we love, like, admire, and/or respect is accused of having engaged in "sexual misconduct."

And just to be clear, at this point in time (late 2017 - early 2018) "sexual misconduct" is the euphemism used for all sexual predatory behavior from a pat on the rear, brushing against a woman's breasts, to forcible rape.

While it is easy to dismiss the seriousness of the pat on the rear or to minimize the brush of an arm or hand against a woman's breast, we do not know how that action affects the woman. And in some cases it is the man who has a woman brush against his genitals or pat his rear.

It makes no difference, both are wrong.

So what can I do about it?

1. Believe the person making the accusation. There is an element of truth in their story. *It is incredibly courageous to speak out even in 2017.*
2. Suspend my judgement as to whether it was "that serious." *It is serious enough to the person speaking out that she or he is willing to risk ridicule, disbelief, threats, etc. and to still speak out.*
3. Support an investigation even if the person being accused is someone I like and respect and especially if the person being accused is someone I love or with whom I have a personal relationship.
4. Use my professional knowledge to educate people around me.
5. Pay attention to the signs of pedophilia such as the process called "grooming" and know that pedophiles have the ability to delay gratification for long periods of time (as in years) while they not only groom the child but also the adults in the child's life.
6. Always teach children that they have the right to say who touches them. Support children who do

not want to hug and kiss someone, even when that someone is me.

Obviously I'm not changing the world or keeping all children safe but I am making a difference in the lives of the children I know and with whom I have contact.

In addition I can support legislation that protects children. I can continue to speak out from a professional position about pedophiles and the importance of adults paying attention to and **believing** the Children.

8

FINDING BALANCE IN A CRAZY WORLD

Now what?

Staying Sane in a Crazy World is also about how to deal with those times when our lives feel (or may actually be) out of balance.

Before you make your *Personal Staying Sane Plan*, ask yourself.

Do I know when my life is *in balance*?

Some people don't have that yardstick measurement and only know when things are out of balance.

Remember, we want our plan to focus on what we want – a sane life. For some of us that means a life in balance.

Time to make another list.

This one details how you know when your life is in balance? Be specific.

My list includes the following:

***Within a narrow time frame (although not necessarily within a 24 hour period of time), I have fun, laugh, do something that brings me joy, engage with people I love, sleep well, take care of mundane or less than fun tasks, spend time outdoors as well as inside, see the beauty of the world around me.

***When my life is in balance, doing the laundry, taking the trash out, going grocery shopping is just something I do. No grumbling, muttering, feet dragging or complaining, I just get whatever it is done.

***When my life is in balance, I spend three to five hours a day writing and the words flow. Social media is something I do. Staying connected to my writer friends is a daily blessing.

When your life is in balance what are you doing?

Where are you?

Who is with you?

How do you feel both emotionally and physically?

It is critical to take the time to identify what your life is like when it is in balance.

Why?

Because staying focused on moving in the direction of how you want your life to be is the easiest way to create that life for yourself.

There are numerous ideas from creating a vision board, posting positive messages at various points around your house, car and work space to help you focus on the positive. If you do not have this message, add it.

Engage in Something Bigger Than Yourself.

Here are some of the things people do that bring them joy and have a positive impact in the lives of others:

Volunteer one day a week or even a half-day. Meals on Wheels always needs volunteers and there are at risk seniors and others who need a ride to appointments, dialysis, etc.

Help a friend. Volunteer to support a friend who is struggling. Calling and checking on your friend, sending a note if they live far away, suggesting a simple outing (walk around the block for example) or sharing a cup of coffee/tea.

There are dozens if not hundreds of places to volunteer. What are you interested in: animals, children, nature, peace, healing?

It is amazing how our own worries and cares fade when we are committed to helping someone else.

You can find a project that is bigger than you right in your neighborhood, town/city or county (maybe even your state). From working in animal shelters to being a foster parent to a four-legged furry friend, reading to children in your local school or volunteering to chaperone field trips and other activities. There will be something that beckons you to join in.

In Oregon we have designated days each year for beach clean-up. There are volunteer crews that work in parks to clear out invasive species. If that's more than you want to commit to, keep a bag with you and pick up litter as you go on a walk or hike.

What ideas do you have? Still not sure? Check out local organizations such as Optimists, Rotary, Elks and other service organizations. Graduated from college? What about your alumni association?

And if nothing already in place speaks to you, start something.

If you haven't seen CNN's Every Day Heroes, do. It is heart-warming, uplifting and shows what can happen when one (1) person sees a need and responds. Here's a link to the 2016 awards show:

http://www.cnn.com/2015/10/08/us/cnn-top-ten-heroes-2015/index.html.

Step outside yourself and experiment.

Find what brings you joy.

During the time you are experimenting, consider whether you will share your experiment with someone else. Of course telling your dog, cat, bird or two month old child is probably safe. Just be particularly aware of what the person you are thinking about revealing your new ideas to might do or say.

Bottom line: What's important is that you find something that brings You joy! Singing in the shower, writing a poem, writing song lyrics, writing a book, painting a picture, taking a picture, planting a flower or a tree or a bush or a shrub.

What brings you joy?

Now add that to your day or maybe it's more realistic to add it to your week. And, if you can't actually engage in the activity, use your imagination to create it in your mind. Remember when you meditate or visualize your brain cannot tell the difference between participating in that action and reality.

9

STAYING SANE SPIRITUAL PRACTICES

Another *Staying Sane* key is to have a spiritual practice. I am not talking about religion. Gratitude, being grateful for something outside yourself is spiritual: the beauty in nature, a sunrise, a sunset, the wonder of seeing a bud turn into a flower, relaxing and feeling grateful for the warm sun while lying by the pool or on the sand.

Depending on your beliefs it could be reading the Bible, attending church on Sunday or more often, or even saying prayers as you go through your day.

For me a spiritual practice is more than going to church and reading a Holy Book. It is about living my Core Values to the best of my ability each day.

What do you believe?

Who shares a similar belief?

When can you spend time together?

Review what you wrote in Chapter Two about Core Values. What might you add to that list?

Here are more of mine

"I believe people are intrinsically good."

"I believe we are all energetically connected and therefore are part of The Whole or The One. Some people might use the word Devine or God. What the connection is named isn't critical to understanding the concept and thus one of my Core Values. Here is an example: if I stub my toe, more than my toe feels it. The pain reverberates through my body and muscles in my arms, shoulders and jaw can clench. A more positive and equally accurate example: When my feet are massaged, muscles throughout my body relax."

"I believe we are all equal under the eyes of God and man."

Because of my work with Dr. William Glasser and the William Glasser Institute International and the William Glasser Institute - US (http://wglasser.com), I also believe

1. The only person we can control is ourselves
2. All behavior is purposeful and is, in the moment, the person's best effort to create something for themselves.
3. We are all internally motivated therefore everything we choose to do is our attempt to

manifest in the real world those multi-sensory thoughts, images and feelings we hold in our mental storehouse.

I also have a daily personal spiritual practice that starts first thing in the morning and is entwined throughout my day until bed time.

My practice starts with me saying a prayer of gratitude as I get out of bed. Before much of the day has passed, I write out ten things for which I'm grateful.

Throughout the day I find something to be grateful for. It may be the kindness of someone toward me or that I witness.

Today, I am grateful for my friend with whom I had lunch at our favorite Thai restaurant. I'm also grateful for the woman who was our waitress and who quietly cleaned up a mess I accidentally made. I'm grateful for the concern for *my* welfare expressed by the other customers. And I'm especially grateful that my efforts to change the PIN number on my debit card was easy and effortless.

As I write this I'm grateful that my neighbor's husband is here and changing out the batteries in my smoke and carbon monoxide detectors (I'd have to stand on something to do that and my balance isn't as great as it once was).

Tonight (and every night) just before I crawl under the covers, I hold my Gratitude Rock and focus on at least one event in the day for which I'm grateful.

Whenever I find my mind running toward the negative,

crazy world, as soon as I catch myself I stop and purposefully turn my thoughts in a different direction—the direction of gratitude.

There have been days (and most likely will be days) when I'm recalibrating myself back to the positive every few minutes. At those times, it's important to stop and see what's going on.

In my case it is usually one of two things:

1. I'm trying to change something over which I have no control.
2. I don't have a good plan for changing something over which I do have control.

Time to stop and assess what's going on.
Find my footing and move forward again.
As part of finding my footing and moving forward, I use my spiritual practice. And, as already mentioned, expressing gratitude is at the center. Even negative events in my life can be seen with gratitude because: it contrasts the positive; mirrors what I need to work on; and reminds me why I choose to be positive, as well as highlights a life lesson

10

MODIFYING YOUR PLAN
HOW TO DEAL WITH "STUFF" HAPPENING

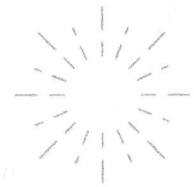

Some of you may be thinking "Wow, this is easy!" Just write out my Core Values, make a list of what I can and cannot control and make a plan to stay positive!

And on the one hand you would be correct. It is simple because the process is very straightforward. Dr. Glasser called this *"The Procedures that Lead To Change."*

What is it you want?

What have you tried? Keep what worked. Modify the 'almost worked'. Toss the rest.

Make a new plan and off you go!

For those of you who are a bit more skeptical, I hear you.

Plans may or may not work, especially if we create a plan that depends on someone else to show up and do something.

And "stuff" happens and throws even good plans off

kilter (think knee deep snow when your plan is to walk a mile every day).

But that doesn't mean we've failed.

One of the key things I learned from Dr. Glasser is that if I am a successful, happy person, I stop and assess what happened, take responsibility for it and then adjust my plan and continue.

Knee deep snow? If we have a step counter, we can walk around and around and around our home until we reach the same number of steps. That's assuming we've tracked how many steps are in that mile – but of course we would have <smile>.

We can give ourselves some 'credit' if we clear off a bit of our deck/porch/walkway. Maybe not all the way down to the ground if it is really knee deep, but even moving a few inches of snow will give us a cardio-workout.

Some things to think about:

View athletes, musicians and artists just before they perform and you'll often see them close their eyes, maybe see a hand move or perhaps it's their head. What they are doing is something you can do. They've learned that visualizing their performance and a successful end result before they even start enhances the probability of their success.

Visualization and meditation are methods that, when you are engaged in them, your brain can't tell the method from reality.

Here's something else to think about.

When you hug someone not only do you and the person you hug feel better; but anyone who observes the hug gets a positive boost of endorphins, our body's natural-high-drug. That is also true for other kind actions we do for each other.

Genuinely thank the wait staff at the restaurant and the other customers see that and get a hit of endorphins.

Here is a fun list:

What are three things you can do regularly to spread positive energy around your home, family, neighborhood or even the world?

Something else to think about:

Because we are human, we are creative. Perhaps not all of us are artistic but something as simple as walking across a floor is a creative activity because we do not walk across the floor exactly the same way every time.

Take a moment and consider that statement. Do you really think our feet hit in the exact same spot on the floor every time we walk across it? Even if we try, there are small discrepancies in our steps.

Accept that because you are human and creative you will do something slightly different. See that is good. Allow yourself the freedom of creativity!

11

WISDOM TO CHOOSE YOUR PATH

And last, we ask for The Wisdom To Know The Difference.

Why is that important? Because, if we are expending a lot of time, effort and energy on something over which we have no control we may be too exhausted, too depleted to work on those things over which we do have control.

The challenge in this is that there are so many things/people over which we **want** control.

My best friend and I used to talk about how much better the world would be if everyone lived by our beliefs, by our Core Values.

As I write this book, around the world people fear terrorist attacks. Terrorists and their jihad against the West are said to be evil. They are described as extremists who want to do away with all other forms of religions so that their way of looking at the world is the only one.

We all **know** that if everyone else believed and did as we believe and do, the world would be a better place.

However, on some level we know that isn't likely to happen. There are numerous examples of people choosing death rather than submit or give in to whomever is holding the literal gun to their head.

Take a moment to reflect on your own Core Values in this area. Are you like the jihadist*** who believes that there is only one way to live in the world? Only one set of Core Values that all of us should live by?

And reflect on the really hard questions:

How are you different from the jihadist?

What lengths will you go to try to make everyone live by your Core Values?

Remember Dr. William Glasser's Choice Theory concept: All behavior is purposeful and it is our best attempt in that moment to create in the real world a match to that internal picture we have of how we want the world to be. But he also says "The Only Person We Can Control Is Ourselves."

***Merriam-Webster definition of jihad. **Definition** of **jihad.** 1 : a holy war waged on behalf of Islam as a religious duty; also : a personal struggle in devotion to Islam especially involving spiritual discipline. 2 : **a crusade for a principle or belief.**

12

CHANGE AND THE GRIEVING PROCESS

Inherent in all change is loss. You cannot change anything without the loss of something else. That vacation in the Bahama's means you aren't in Hawaii or hiking Machu Picchu much less snuggled in your own bed.

Be prepared that when you change the way you handle stress and take control of your sanity, there will be consequences. Some so minor you may not even recognize it however some may knock you off your path to change.

You could have a friend or group of friends in real life, on Facebook, or other places with whom you've ranted and raved about the injustices of the world. Your Personal Staying Sane Plan may have you leaving ranting and raving behind and opting for another way to deal with the insanity you see.

Yes, it's possible friends, family and acquaintances will see you as giving up, caving in or even betraying them and The Cause.

And that's why we're talking about the Grieving Process.

Elizabeth Kubler Ross's *Death: The Final Stage of Growth* or her *On Death and Dying* are seminal works. I highly recommend Ms. Ross's work if you want to delve into the grieving process.

To be clear, in our case, we aren't talking about a physical death but a non-physical death. We've chosen to make a change which means even though we are excited about our future, there is still a loss of what we have now. Even if we eagerly look forward to the change, there will be some elements that we will miss.

Those elements equal a personal loss. However there is another or "other" loss.

The difference?

Personal: we no longer engage with the outside world in the same way.

Other: involves "others" and because we are not interacting in the same way, other people feel the loss.

Some losses are minor and we feel a twinge of sadness or regret. I remember going through my closet when I retired and pulling out all my professional suits and dresses. Yes, I was donating them to the Dress For Success program so that part felt good but...

No longer having these clothes truly meant I was retired.

And some of those clothes were favorites. I loved the color, feel of the fabric, etc. That was a little loss. I dealt with my feelings through reminiscing about certain events when I wore this or that or where I bought it. I treated myself to a tasty treat because I'd stuck with the task until it was done—the closet cleared out and the bags of clothes were in the trunk of my car.

That was pretty much it. A bit of sadness and some wistfulness as I sorted through memories. This loss also only impacted me for a short time because I wasn't sad or wistful for long.

A significant loss was when my last dog, Duke, went to doggie heaven. He was a wonderful dog, faithful, loved me unconditionally and unless there was a cat around, he always came when called. (I'm smiling as I write that last sentence.)

He was old, had lung cancer, doggie dementia and was often incontinent. He became so stressed whenever I left the house because he couldn't find me. He'd wander around looking for me, sometimes just standing at the bottom of the stairs he could no longer climb as if expecting me to appear.

Making the decision to no longer take him with me was hard on both of us. But he had trouble getting into and out of the car, then there was the possible incontinency in the car. Memories of the ten years he was with me are bittersweet. He was a wonderfully fantastic dog and I miss him still. Not wistful sadness but a deep longing. There are times I call upon his ghost to come and haunt my yard and chase the squirrels and cats away. So far he's having too good a time in doggie heaven to do so.

The intensity of our grieving process shows us the importance of the loss. If our grief is mild, short-lived and easily put aside, that doesn't mean we haven't experienced it. Of course the deep, overwhelming sense of loss is what we remember as I do my dog.

A brief aside about physical death. You may already know there are cultural, societal and family norms we may feel compelled to follow.

I find it interesting that there was a time when how you dealt with the death of family depended on your place in society? If you know your history, you remember that in the past there was requisite year of mourning when the women wore sober colors and retired from social events such as parties and dancing. Men wore black armbands or ties.

Of course that was true for the more wealthy, privileged classes because the working people couldn't afford to spend the money on an entire new wardrobe in black and somber colors or miss working.

What's also interesting to me is that I've known people who believe if they are happy after the death of someone they love, that's being disrespectful.

But back to the topic of how change triggers grief.

Have you made peace with the loss you will experience when you make the change?

What about the people around you that may be affected by your choices?

Do you have a plan on how to communicate the upcoming changes to minimize the grieving process for you and the other people affected?

Do you understand why someone else would be upset about a change you are making?

Here's why they do:

The people around us have an image of us in their minds. That image has all kinds of assumptions built into it. And one of those assumptions is that we will remain as we've always been.

When we make a change, especially one that's dramatic such as going back to school when our youngest child starts kindergarten, having a complete make-over at the spa with a new hair style, make-up, etc. or quitting a job to start a business, getting a divorce, getting married, moving away—this list can be very long. It really doesn't matter what the change is; it's how you and other's perceive it that counts.

The Grieving Process starts with **Denial.**

Anger is the second stage.

Followed by **Depression.**

Hope/Bargaining is the fourth stage and hang-in there because the final stage is **Acceptance.**

Let's look at the Grieving Process in a bit more detail using the classic examples of death and dying as well as the changes we're going to make as we regain our sanity.

Denial: Usually a brief period of time where we deny something is even wrong. We see that when someone dies and the first reaction is "No, that can't be."

Reminding ourselves that it is true – our spouse did just walk out, the marriage is over, the job is lost, the company filed for bankruptcy that morning. Whatever the "death" is can take time to assimilate the change.

What also impacts **Denial** is whether we have the ability to think in the abstract. Once we understand the concept of time, we think in the abstract. While I'm speaking primarily to adults who can think in the abstract, you may be around young children who have yet to develop abstract thinking.

A rule of thumb is if a child can comprehend time (not the big hand points in one direction and the little hand in another or even knowing the number) they can comprehend abstracts. Talking to a child in specific concrete terms is the only way to help a small child move out of denial.

In our case, you may find people ignore you and the change. They may continue to engage with you as if nothing has changed and attempt to draw you in to the way you used to respond to events. More likely you'll see the second stage in some form.

Anger: In divorce or abandonment, as soon as the realization that the other party is gone hits, **anger** is a normal reaction. In death, it's there but often suppressed. In Western society, being angry at someone who has just died is often misunderstood. And if we don't understand this step in the grieving process when we hear statements or questions such as "Why did she have to die and leave me alone?" or "I don't know if I can even take care of everything like he did." We may not understand that this is an expression of **anger.**

Anger in our case may show up as other people berating us for abandoning them, changing sides and becoming "one of them." There are numerous examples on the evening news of people expressing anger because their core values are threatened.

When we push aside, deny or suppress this second stage in the grieving process, we create long term problems. Because our anger can or even is frightening to us and we cover it over with the third phase.

Depression There are millions of people diagnosed with depression and on medication around the world. Obviously medication isn't the answer because people are on these drugs often for the rest of their lives.

What's important here is that **depression** is a normal step in the grieving process. And when the grief is over a life event that seems small or inconsequential we may not even understand where our grief/depression originates.

That low-level, just under the surface dissatisfaction with life is a major cause of **depression.** Feeling trapped or overwhelmed by issues over which we have no control can also create a sense of hopelessness which is a classic symptom of **depression.**

We may not really understand how anyone could resent

our taking better care of ourselves. We may not be prepared for the angry words spew our way.

In some cases we'll feel down and not immediately able to put our finger on what's wrong. However before we can move forward past the **anger** and **depression**, we must pay attention and figure out what we are grieving about. Once we do that, we can work on a resolution so we can continue through the grieving process to—

Hope/Bargaining: "Maybe if I'd" or "If only I'd" (fill in the blank) are ways of trying to put things back the way they were. If we lose our job when the company downsizes, it isn't uncommon for us to wonder "Maybe if I'd—". Hindsight is always 20/20 but we live in the present. *We also bounce between anger "it isn't fair or right" and depression "what am I going to do now?"*

When we bargain in the present we often call upon our spirituality. People ask for help, for guidance, for salvation, for a way out of the mess. They bargain by offering future changes if only things change for the better.

In a divorce kids can spend years in this stage. I even know of situations where children have held out hope for their parents to reunite even after one or both of them remarried.

In our situation, we're making a decision to change. However, if we have people in our lives who are not supportive, we most likely will be thinking maybe there is something we can do so we don't lose the relationship.

Acceptance: comes when we reach that point when we realize that nothing is going to change and we make peace with our "new normal". Our spouse has died and is not coming back, the company closed and the job is lost, the landlord sold our house and we must move, we can't see well without our glasses. In our case, we are well on our new path and there are some friends, family and acquaintances who have not accepted the new us.

Once we accept that the change is now a fact, we begin to look at our world and our life from this new perspective.

Since this is a process, we sometimes jump around from stage to stage. We're out of anger and into depression and then something happens and we're angry all over again. **Acceptance?** Yes, finally we sigh and relax. Oops, back in depression or anger or even hope/bargaining.

My dad died in March 1998 and while I don't experience a deep depression, I do experience a bittersweet, wistful feeling when I'm on a walk and see a beautiful garden. In that moment I miss him and wish he was with me.

The same is true for my mom, who passed in March 2002, when I'm enjoying my great grands. She loved children and she'd have been reading books and telling stories, rocking them to sleep.

And I've already shared about my Duke.

I worked in Social Services for over fifty years. There are times when that wistful feeling, that reflects the loss of the satisfaction I gained from that work, is strong.

More recently, I spent most of a year assisting a friend whose wife had died. I'm glad I did. However, I lost most of a year of my writing life.

Why am I belaboring an early point? Because it is critically important to understand that as you create *Your Personal Staying Sane Plan,* you are changing and those changes have consequences to you personally and in your relationship with others.

When feelings about those changes are strong, that's a signal to pay attention to the grieving process, to the fact that you might not even realize the level of attachment you have to the present situation, person, item or belief. However, if the feelings are more subtle, you may become mired in that low-grade dissatisfaction with your life. And, that will weaken your commitment to the new direction you've chosen.

Staying Sane in a Crazy World is focused on Core Values. Know that means our belief systems are subject to loss and thus to grief.

Here are some examples from the lives of the heroines in The Sacred Women's Circle series.

Lily: The Dragon and The Great Horned Owl and Hunter: The Dancer and The Drum

In these two stories the heroines, Lily and Hunter share a Core Value or Belief that if she is strong, independent and self-sufficient, she is safe. Safety guarantees they are not vulnerable. And that belief of invincibility is a myth therefore they each come face-to-face with that reality.

Fears and doubts surface and are exacerbated when they are faced with the men of their dreams because loving another is the most vulnerable spot of all. Their stories are about them finding their way through chaos and challenges to their happily-ever-after.

Diana: The Queen of Swords and The Knight of Pentacles and *Ashley: Dragonflies and Dreams*

Diana's marriage may have initially been based on love but it is now solely one of maintaining image. Ashley's physical beauty was praised all of her life.

Both women are caught in the "image is everything" trap. Diana now in an abusive marriage and Ashley in making choices that can endanger her life in an effort to keep her marriage intact.

How do you find and honor who you are under the surface? How do you accept a beauty that comes from your essence? How do you change a life-time belief that no longer serves you?

And from my own life:

I was raised to believe if I worked hard for my employer and did my very best, I would be rewarded and recognized for my efforts. In reality that didn't happen.

When I was injured on the job taking abandoned children into protective custody, I carried on with the tasks of placement, reports and court hearing the next morning.

Long story short—months later I hired an attorney to protect myself as my employer did not protect me from the insurance company.

The death of that belief was hard and I struggled through all stages of the grieving process. After all I'd been an excellent employee for over ten years (just look at my performance evaluations).

The destruction of that deep seated belief, in some ways, was more devastating than the physical injury (which is bothering me today – go figure).

In *Love, Power, Freedom, Fun: How To Get More,* we take a look at the Grieving Process in more depth. Included in that book, due out Winter 2019, are exercises to assist you to more fully understand how you personally deal with grief.

13

REVISIT YOUR CORE VALUES

This is a place to stop and take a look at where we stand on the continuum of life. Are we at the *live and let live* end or are we at the *everyone must be/believe/live as I do.*

How does this continuum fit with our Core Values?

It's one thing to say you are at the live and let live end when it comes to what pizza to order; but what about when your Core Values are involved?

An environmentalist who sees the old growth forest as sacred and thus knows no trees should be cut down.

A parent who knows what's best for their child and thus knows how this child should live his/her life including profession and spouse.

Business owners who are convinced they must be

successful (make money) thus they do "whatever it takes" to make money.

A person of (insert a faith) who believes and thus knows this is The True Faith and it is their responsibility to bring everyone else into the fold.

While we may not use the word "jihad" to describe us when we are at the "everyone should believe and live as I do" end of the continuum, given the second definition it would be appropriate.

And if using the word "jihad" gives you pause? Hopefully it is not enough to keep you from finishing this book, and crafting your Personal Staying Sane Plan.

The great religions of the world are founded on tolerance and love, caring for each other, showing kindness and compassion. Taking care of those who are unable (for whatever reason) to care for themselves.

So as I come to the end of *Staying Sane in a Crazy World*, I invite you to go back and review your Core Values.

Over the years, as I've talked to people about their values/beliefs, there are some I hear spoken of on a regular basis. I've included some of them below. As you read through them you will see that I pose both sides. I do that because I've heard both sides.

What I know is true is that whichever side of the value you believe, it impacts or determines what you see as "crazy."

What I also know is true is we become fearful when we perceive our Core Values are attacked. That is especially true if we do not have as a Core Value that everyone has a right to their point of view (belief).

As I've mentioned above people are willing to die for a Core Value. We call these people extremists and martyrs and saints. But they are in many ways no different than us. They have a Core Value and they want the rest of the world to hold and to live by that same Core Value.

As you read each of the following Core Values, ask yourself how you live this Core Value in your daily life.

Do you believe "love thy neighbor as thyself" or "thou who art without sin throw the first stone"?

Do you believe love conquers all?

Do you believe the "all men are created equal" of the US Constitution?

Do you believe in a loving God or a loving Higher Power, Spirit?

Do you believe you attract more of what you want with "honey" than with "vinegar?"

Do you believe that people are inherently good or inherently evil?

Do you view the glass of the world as half-full or half-empty?

Do you believe everyone *has a right* to be safe, educated, have food, shelter clothing or must they *earn* or in some way show they *deserve* education, food, housing, etc.?

Do people who've made poor or bad choices have a right to a second chance?

Can people be "rehabilitated" if they have committed a crime, become addicted to a legal or illegal substance?

Do you hold the Core Values of the United States (if you are a resident herein) as stated in The Constitution and The Bill of Rights as your own Values?

And if you've not read The Constitution and The Bill of Rights since high school, you may want to refresh your memory before you answer.

Here are links:

The Constitution:

https://www.archives.gov/founding-docs/constitution

The Bill of Rights:

https://www.archives.gov/founding-docs/bill-of-rights-transcript

14

MY PERSONAL STAYING SANE PLAN

I mentioned Dr. William Glasser earlier in this book. These next two chapters are focused on his work.

Dr. William Glasser first came to my attention in the 1960's when a few of my co-workers, attended a "Day With Glasser" lecture based on his book *Reality Therapy*. They'd recorded his talk and brought the audio cassette tapes to the office. I remember crowding around the table in the lunch room listening to him talk about how taking personal responsibility for ourselves was how to change our lives. Heady stuff in the mid-1960's.

I became officially involved in training through The Institute for Reality Therapy (now known as The William Glasser Institute) in August of 1978. I became a member of The Institute's teaching faculty a few years later.

Reality Therapy was first taught using "steps." Those steps were turned into "The Procedures That Lead to Change," a series of questions that are woven together to assist us in finding our way through whatever our problem is to a plan of action.

What follows is "The Procedures that Lead to Change" used in the context of *My Personal Staying Sane Plan*.

WHAT DO I WANT?

1. Do I have control or the ability to affect change?
2. How does what I want fit with my Core Values?
3. Review your answers and assess the language you've used so you are stating what you want from the positive.

What have I already done to get what I want?

1. List even the negative things such as complaining, etc.
2. Where do my Core Values fit in? Have I been in "integrity" with my Core Values or have I strayed?

Review to see if anything has worked even a little or if there is some part of your actions you feel good about.

1. Where do you see yourself living your Core Values?

What's your plan? Your plan can take one of two directions. You continue to strive for what you want regardless of the odds. Or, you make a plan to "Accept The Things I Cannot Change/ Over Which I Have No Control."

A few pointers on making plans that work:

1. Successful plans are dependent only on you the plan-maker. This element of a successful plan is often daunting because what we want is someone else to change!
2. Successful plans are living documents and can be changed if they are not working.
3. Successful plans have specificity: who, what, where, when, how
4. Successful plans are measurable because of the specificity.

At the end of this book, you'll find the details and outline for creating your very own ***Personal Staying Sane Plan***. You can also find a downloadable copy of ***My Personal Staying Sane Plan*** worksheet on my website. http://judithashleyromance.com.

You can learn more about Dr. William Glasser's "Procedures That Lead to Change" by attending a Basic Intensive

Training that leads to Certification in Choice Theory and Reality Therapy through The William Glasser Institute, reading Dr. Glasser's *Choice Theory, Reality Therapy* or any number of his books. Or you may choose to attend a "Take Charge of Your Life" workshop.

Check out http://wglasser.com for more information. New workshops, trainings, books and other products are being developed and added as I write this. And, if you have an area of your life you'd like specifically addressed, please let The William Glasser Institute know. http://wglasser.com

Remember that the craziness we see and feel comes when our own Core Values are threatened. Since we can only control ourselves (although we may influence someone with the information we share with them), when we stay true to our Core Values by living them each day, we have the highest possibility of Staying Sane no matter how crazy the world around us becomes.

May you find peace in your body, heart and soul as you find your path to living your Core Values every day.

In love and light,

Judith

15

STAYING SANE - UPDATE

If you recall, in Chapter One I wrote that it was September 2017 when I started *Staying Sane in a Crazy World*. It is now late February, 2018 and while I'm on the cusp of publishing this book, I'm not quite there.

Since I started this book, here in the United States we have experienced devastating natural disasters like hurricanes, earthquakes, flooding, blizzards and fires. In addition world-wide there are the man-made disasters like images from wars fought out on our news most nights, mass shootings and bombings.

If that isn't enough there are the lesser known disasters like the DUI driver that kills a father, mother or child. The lives involved might total a miniscule number of our US population much less the world's population but the effects are no less shattering.

And our world can be turned upside down by a simple personal experience. That project you put your heart and soul into, that was the best you could do, fails.

That challenging task you finished and forever crossed off your "to do" list pops back to life.

Since I am a relatively fast typist and this isn't the first book I've written, what has taken so long?

LIFE has intervened and thus this chapter.

Just because you have training and a skill set, a *Personal Staying Sane Plan* doesn't mean you'll never experience the challenge of losing your grip when the world goes crazy.

However, because you do have a *My Personal Staying Sane Plan*, you have the power to regain any lost sanity and move forward.

This chapter is about how I most recently used my own *Personal Staying Sane Plan*.

Rather than detail my day-by-day challenges over the past several months ending with more than one Core Value threatened or assaulted, I'll cut to what happened that I stopped and wrote this chapter.

I heard myself question my ability to write this book.

"Who am I to write this book?" That's when I knew I needed to check *My Personal Staying Sane Plan*! Obviously what I was doing wasn't working if I was in a negative, complaining, criticizing place.

The first thing I did after admitting that what I was doing wasn't working was to see what was working. I knew I wanted to continue to start and end my day with "Gratitude."

Obviously that wasn't enough.

I took some time and focused positive, healing energy to the world in accordance with my core value that we are all connected and if one of us is hurt, it hurts us all.

I also looked at what I have control over and what I don't.

I do have control over me. I do not have control over anyone else.

I have control over how I respond to disasters and tragedies. Since I have a core value that people are entitled to their point of view, to live by that means I make an effort to not engage in rants or soap box oratory. *It does not mean I have no opinion or that I do not express it. It does mean I choose my words in an attempt to not add to the polarization on a topic.*

I have control over what, how and if I engage in any discussion of any of the natural or manmade disasters I'm aware of.

I can check my own "fear level." As a trauma survivor myself, I'm aware when events that demolish my peace and serenity occur, my own PTSD (Post Traumatic Stress Disorder) can be heightened. Double-checking what's real as in what is happening right now versus could or couldn't happen is important.

My body is a great communicator to my brain and I rely

on its signals while monitoring the "what's real and what's not real" aspect of the messages.

The above was a process that I went through over a 24 hour period of time. I checked and double-checked my plan against my own physical, visceral reactions to each aspect.

In the end I decided to curtail my intake of news both from television and social media. To up the number of times I say "thank you" to myself and others each day. To be especially kind and gentle with myself. Here are a few of the things I've done for myself.

I've treated myself to doing nothing "productive," putting off tasks to another day, rescheduling appointments that don't "feel" right (remember I rely on my body to be a better communicator in some things than my brain), to ask for help even if I could probably do it myself, to talk to friends when I just need to get the words out of my head into the world.

As you've seen in the *My Personal Staying Sane Plan* form, I've included *My Revised Personal Staying Sane Plan*. This chapter is why. We have no control over what others do, we can only control ourselves. We are responsible for our sanity and by using the information in this book, you can take control of your life, find what works for you and live a happier and healthier life.

Because the truth is, if everyone in the entire world made the decision to respect the Core Values of every other person, to live a peaceful life, to resolve all differences by peaceful means the need for *My Personal Staying Sane Plan* would be negligible.

16

EXAMPLE: JUDITH'S STAYING SANE PLAN - 02/2018

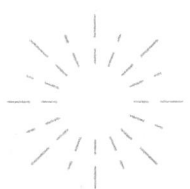

My Core Values affected:

- All life is sacred.
- If one of us is hurt, we are all hurt.
- Violence solves nothing.
- Peaceful means can solve all problems if everyone involved wants a peaceful outcome.

What I can control but don't:
In this situation I have no control and I was not directly involved.

What I can control:
My response in thought, word and deed to the situation.

What I can't control entirely but can still do something about:

- I can model what I want to happen.
- I can support others who have more direct control over the situation.

What I can't control:

- What other people do when upset, angry, frustrated.
- What businesses do to make a profit regardless of the cost.

What my "letting go" plan is: (The crux of your plan. What are you doing to let go of those things over which you have no control and therefore cannot change)?

What I am doing to let go of the things over which I have no control is

- Take a deep breath and remind myself that this is not something over which I have control.
- Trust that all is happening in right time.
- Be aware of what is happening so if there is something I can do, some action I can take, I am prepared.

My do plan: (What I'm going to do).

- Limit my exposure to the news, especially the pictures. I may choose to listen to the news rather than watch because I want to know what is happening.
- Increase my own practice of Gratitude.
- Pay attention to how I feel physically because my body is usually more perceptive than my brain.
- Give myself permission to cancel or reschedule any and all appointments until I'm doing well.
- Give myself permission to grieve.
- Send love and light into the world at least twice a day.

ANOTHER FORMAT OPTION FOR MY STAYING SANE PLAN

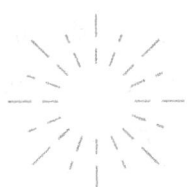

My Plan:

What I am going to do:

- *Monitor my news intake*
- *Increase my practice of Gratitude*
- *Pay attention to how I feel physically because my body is usually more perceptive than my brain.*
- *Give myself permission to cancel or reschedule any and all appointments until I'm doing well.*
- *Give myself permission to grieve.*
- *Send love and light into the world at least twice a day.*

Why I am doing it:

I want to physically, emotionally and mentally feel more balanced.

When I'm going to do it.
Starting now, February 22, 2018.

How I'm going to do it.
I've written down my plan and posted it on the kitchen refrigerator, the front door and by "my chair." I've shared my plan with two friends because I know I'm more likely to follow through when I share my plan publicly.

My SEES time frame.

- *I will initially evaluate this plan at the end of every day or more often if I feel more distressed and off-balance.*
- *If it seems to be working after three days, I'll extend my evaluation plan to every other day.*
- *I'll follow the extending the evaluation as long as it seems to be working.*
- *If I need to, I'll use the* **My Revised Plan** *outline.*

EXAMPLE: MY REVISED PLAN:
WHAT I'M GOING TO DO DIFFERENTLY

Why I think this change will help me be successful

How/When I'm going to implement the change.

MY SEES time frame.

CRITERIA FOR A GOOD PLAN
A GOOD PLAN IS HOW YOU MAKE STAYING SANE YOUR REALITY

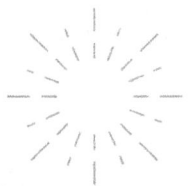

I use the following criteria to ensure my success because I've learned how important it is to have all the components of my plan work together.

A Good Plan Is

Simple: Something that is easy to do.

Measurable: You know if you've don't it or not.

Attainable: You believe you can do it.

Dependent Only On You: You can do it no matter what anyone else is doing.

A Good Plan Has A

Who: That would be you. All plans are in the first person "My plan... ."

What: What are you going to do? Pretty much a restatement of A Good Plan Is.

Why: What benefit do you see for yourself when you complete this plan?

How: How are you going to accomplish your plan? What are the steps you need to take to be successful in completing your plan?

When: What is your time frame for starting and completing this plan?

Where: Where will this plan take place? (home, school, community, etc.)

A Good Plan Maker (That would also be you) SEES:

Sets specific times to assess how the plan is working

Evaluates the plan rather than criticizing or blaming self or others.

Explores ways to modify the plan if there are problems

Seeks advice or input from others to craft a reviews plan as needed.

20

YOUR PERSONAL STAYING SANE PLAN

CLICK TITLE FOR DOWNLOAD LINK

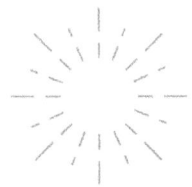

My Core Values: (You can list words or phrases but the more details you include the more effective your plan will be).

What I can control but don't: (These are the tasks related to your core values that you can do but for a variety of reasons, don't).

What I can control: (The easy one. These are the things you can control and do take action on).

What I can't control entirely but can still do something about: (Remember my examples around the environment and politics)?

What I can't control: (Someone else's choices, another country's decisions, the weather are some examples).

What my "letting go" plan is: (The crux of your plan. What are you doing to let go of those things over which you have no control and therefore cannot change)?

21

ALTERNATIVE FORMAT FOR YOUR PERSONAL STAYING SANE PLAN

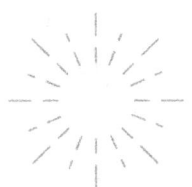

Why is this section duplicated? Because I've given you two different formats from which to craft your *Personal Staying Sane Plan*. Whichever one you use, be sure to go through this section and make sure all your components are in alignment with "A Good Plan Is" because **A good plan is how you make Staying Sane your reality.**

A Good Plan Is
Simple: Something that is easy to do.
Measurable: You know if you've don't it or not.
Attainable: You believe you can do it.

Dependent Only On You: You can do it no matter what anyone else is doing.

A Good Plan Has A

Who: That would be you. All plans are in the first person "My plan… ."

What: What are you going to do? Pretty much a restatement of A Good Plan Is.

Why: What benefit do you see for yourself when you complete this plan?

How: How are you going to accomplish your plan? What are the steps you need to take to be successful in completing your plan?

When: What is your time frame for starting and completing this plan?

Where: Where will this plan take place? (home, school, community, etc.)

A Good Plan Maker (That would also be you) SEES:

Sets specific times to assess how the plan is working

Evaluates the plan rather than criticizing or blaming self or others.

Explores ways to modify the plan if there are problems
Seeks advice or input from others to craft a reviews plan as needed.

And because plans are often/usually imperfect, I've included the outline for the next step.

My Revised Plan:

What I'm going to do differently

Why I think this change will help me be successful

How/When I'm going to implement the change.

My SEES time frame.

BONUS MATERIAL

Where Do Core Values Come From?
The Basic Needs

Dr. William Glasser first came to the notice of mental health and corrections professionals when his book *Reality Therapy* was published in the 1960's. It was considered radical and his ideas were not well accepted within the psychiatric community.

In *Reality Therapy* and his "Day with Dr. Glasser" presentations he talked about the importance of relationships. He described and then demonstrated through role plays with audience members that Reality Therapy was a co-creation process that relied on therapists and clients working together. The role of the therapist was to assist clients in clarifying what they wanted and help them create a plan that had a high probability of success.

This different approach and the problem-solving process outlined earlier in *Staying Sane* worked not only in formal therapeutic relationships but also in other situations such as corrections (jails, prisons, parole and probation), education (schools at all grade levels), work places (employee-customer, employee-supervisor or employee-employee) and parenting to name a few.

It worked because of the shift in responsibility from the top-down person (therapist, parole officer, employer, teacher, parent) telling the client, parolee, employee, student, child what must done to inviting them to participate in the process. This critical difference in how the people who were in powerless positions were treated made a significant difference in their being able to participate in creating a plan that worked for them.

The foundation for *Reality Therapy* and later *Choice Theory: A New Psychology of Personal Freedom* is the genetically encoded Five Basic Needs (Survival, Love, Power, Freedom, Fun). Discontent, unhappiness, misery comes from either those needs being in conflict with one another or our circumstances reduce our ability to fully meet one or more of those needs.

I've included my paraphrasing and summary of Dr. Glasser's thinking on the concept that these Five Basic Needs are genetically encoded in our DNA. Do read *Choice Theory:*

A New Psychology of Personal Freedom for a more in depth explanation.

First comes *Survival.* Most of us would agree that we have a need to survive, to have adequate food, shelter, clothing, safety so that we can continue life. Included in survival is procreation (sex) as that element ensures the continuation of the species. You might think that survival is the foundation of the needs as Abraham Maslow's Hierarchy of Needs suggests, however, in Glasser's Choice Theory, the Basic Needs are genetically encoded so they are not in a hierarchy and they are as individual to each of us as is our hair and eye color.

Throughout time, we have learned it is easier to survive if we band together. Even today it is easier and even essential in meeting our other basic needs to have other people in our lives. Being physically close to other people allows us to more easily develop friendly attachments. And those friendly attachments grow into love. All of our other basic needs are enhanced through our ability to meet our Basic Need of *Love, Belonging, Relationships.*

The Basic Need most challenging for us to meet is *Power, Competence, Mastery, Importance.* Power comes in two forms – Power Over and Personal Power. Virtually all of us have experienced a time where someone has Power Over us. It could be a boss who is inappropriate or cruel but we need the job in order to support ourselves and/or our family. It could be a spouse who says the (to me) dreadful words "If you loved me, you would —." If staying in this marriage is important to you for any reason, your spouse is now in a Power Over position.

Power Over destroys relationships because whatever means necessary are employed (criticism, nagging, threatening, punishing, etc.) to make the other person do what we want. Glasser calls that External Control Psychology or ECP.

From a Choice Theory point of view, ECP is the basis for all the problems in the world and stems from the belief that I know better than you what's best for you. In addition to knowing better, Power Over people are always "right." And last but not least is what I want is more important than what you want.

While ECP is the Power Over side of the Basic Need for Power, the other side the equation is Personal Power. Personal Power is about how we feel when we excel at a task, are seen by others as competent or where we are sought out by others for our input or advice.

Someone with a strong need for Personal Power is usually seen as an excellent leader or manager. People want to work with this person for the good of the family, company or society. As a group we set a goal and strive to meet it.

Or we may not set the goal but we have direct input as to the best way to meet it. The best jobs I've had over the years gave me a lot of personal power in getting the tasks accomplished.

As parents we may decide to landscape the yard but

using Personal Power as our base, we'll include all family members in the design and implementation.

Certain *Freedom*s are guaranteed in the United States Bill of Rights. As most know, our founding fathers were wealthy, aristocratic educated men (some of whom were atheists) from England. They chafed at a system that pigeon-holed them and thus traveled across the Atlantic Ocean (or were first or second generation born in the US) to gain a measure of freedom.

In writing the Bill of Rights, they wanted to ensure that the freedoms they sought (speech, religion, etc.) were protected. They also wanted the fledgling U.S. to be able to protect itself from invaders which is why the right to form a militia and bear arms is included.

Because of these Freedoms people from around the world have looked to the United States as a beacon of opportunity. A place where they could speak their truth, worship (or not) as they chose, etc.

The need for Freedom does not necessarily co-exist well with the need for Love nor with the need for Power. As Dr. Glasser writes, many wars are fought in the name of Freedom but the underlying issue is Power. As I write this the world is in turmoil as various religions fight for the right to force everyone to believe their tenets and live in the manner proscribed by their religious laws. All sides are in a Power Over position. As the Bill of Rights guarantees we each are free to believe and worship (or not) as we wish, only

Personal Power fits what our founding fathers wanted to protect with the Bill of Rights.

Certainly the last of these needs is not the most unimportant. **Fun** may be seen as frivolous but fun has been critically important as we've evolved. In early stages of life, fun is how we learn to walk, talk, play house, school and store. Fun brings smiles and laughter and an innate knowing of a truth hidden in a joke.

While we watch videos of lion cubs stalking and pouncing on the lioness's tail, we see them practicing skills they'll need to survive as adults.

I easily recall the delight I felt as my son, granddaughters and great grands learned to turn over, then crawl and finally walk, learn to ride a bike, etc. The look of astonishment when they mastered the skill, the joy that shone on their faces remain some of my treasured memories.

How many times have you sung the "ABC Song"? I'm in the multiple thousands I'm sure. Learning through song and games is easier than rote learning unless you are someone like me who equates memorizing with Personal Power.

To summarize further:

While **Survival** is important, people do suicide and risk their lives for Love, Power, Freedom and Fun. They also risk disease which can lead to death to have indiscriminate sex.

Yes, **Love, Belonging and Relationships** are important to our survival and our ability to meet our need for Power, Freedom and Fun. And yet, people destroy relationships in order to be in a Power Over position, as well as to meet their Freedom and Fun needs.

Power, Mastery, Competence and Importance is comprised of both Power Over and Personal Power. Power Over is seductive in that people who thrive on this need feel even more powerful when dominating others. Misery for those in the Powerless position can be dangerous (think of uprising, riots, etc.). From my perspective leading from a position of Personal Power takes more skill and confidence than ruling from Power Over.

Freedom, Movement and Choice? How free can we be if we are in a relationship with someone who wants us to be with them all the time or at least more than we want? And, if we truly believe in Freedom as a right, how do we justify our attempts to control others? We all have a myriad of choices we make every day. Not all of them are easy choices. In fact, there are times some of the things we do, don't feel like choices at all.

Fun, Laughter, Learning. If you are a risk taker, you may already understand the seductive allure of dangerous **Fun**. Dangerous fun butts up against our Survival need and can also impact our Love, Belonging and Relationship need. I love to learn and laugh but I can't imagine bungee jumping much less watching a horror movie or reading a thriller.

In order to have the life we want to live, understanding how our Basic Needs are encoded in our DNA is important. My newest book ***Love, Power, Freedom, Fun: How To Get More*** is slated to be released before the end of 2018. It starts with exercises to assist you to determine the strength of your Basic Needs and how well they are being met.

By the end, if you complete the exercises, you'll be well on your way to *How To Get More*.

NEW NON-FICTION BY JUDITH ASHLEY

Coming Winter 2019
  Love, Power, Fun, Freedom: How To Get More

Coming Spring 2019
  Sacred Women's Circle Prayers and Ceremony

Interested in being the first to know what Judith is up to? What new books are coming out and when?
  Yes, sign me up!
  https://app.convertkit.com/landing_pages/134583?v=7

FICTION BY JUDITH ASHLEY

The Sacred Women's Circle series

Lily: The Dragon and the Great Horned Owl

Elizabeth: The Lady and the Sacred Grove

Diana: The Queen of Swords and the Knight of Pentacles

Ashley: Dragonflies and Dreams

Hunter: The Drum and The Dance

Gabriella: Chaos to Symmetry

Sophia: Every Ending Is A Beginning

Visions of Happiness: A Sacred Women's Circle novel

CONNECT WITH JUDITH

Learn more by checking out

Judith's website at http://judithashleyromance.com

Judith's Windtree Press Author Page at
https://windtreepress.com/judith-ashley-2/

Follow Judith on these Social Media sites:

Judith's Facebook page
https://www.facebook.com/JudithAshley.Romance

Judith's Twitter page
https://twitter.com/JudithAshley19

You can also keep up with Judith each Monday when Judith's weekly blog is at

http://judithashley.blogspot.com

Support your indie author by leaving a review on your favorite e-retailer or social media.

ACKNOWLEDGMENTS

Because of issues in my own life, at times writing this book was a struggle. Thank you to the wisdom of the #ftb group, my Dark Moon sisters and my friends Paul and Michele for listening to me talk my way through to the end.

More thanks to author Barbara Rae Robinson for reading a very rough draft and giving me feedback. To my Master Mind Sisters Gimi and Connie for reading an earlier draft and their encouragement. And to Maggie Lynch who volunteered to give this book one last read through before I send it off to you.

And everyone who just listened as I rambled on, clarifying as I talked about my ideas, and still encouraged me, you were and are a gift.

As a verbal processor, there'd be no *Staying Sane* without each of you.

ABOUT JUDITH

From Nursery to Nursing Home

In her 50 plus years working in social services, there isn't much Judith Ashley hasn't seen or experienced. In *Staying Sane in a Crazy World,* she draws upon what she has observed work in the lives of people from all walks of life as well as what's worked in her own.

Drawing from the wisdom of "The Serenity Prayer" and the concepts of world-renown psychiatrist Dr. William Glasser, Judith has crafted a simple process anyone can use to find sanity and make peace with what's crazy in their life and world.

By the end of this book you'll have the tools to create your own personal *Staying Sane Plan* so that when in doubt you choose love and light.

http://www.judithashleyromance.com/

WINDTREE PRESS

For more books from the heart in fiction and non-fiction
please visit Windtree Press

http://windtreepress.com

www.ingramcontent.com/pod-product-compliance
Lightning Source LLC
Chambersburg PA
CBHW050202130526
44591CB00034B/1954